Table of Contents

Introduction

Chapter 1: Understand World for Female Entrepreneurship

Chapter 2: Identify a Suitable Business for a B-O-S-S Woman

Chapter 3: Develop Your Brand

Chapter 4: Understand U.S. Regulations for Businesses

Chapter 5: Learn to Lead

Chapter 6: Networking to Make the Dream Work

Chapter 7: Get Money for the Piggy Bank

Chapter 8: Create a Digital Brand

Chapter 9: Market beyond Digital Screens

Chapter 10: Crunch the Numbers

Chapter 11: Project Growth

Introduction

Women wear invisible capes. Dashing from one commitment to the next, it seems impossible for your seemingly superhuman strength to extend to owning your own business. This book has been written to shatter that myth; to prove that you are the B-O-S-S. The female B-O-S-S is a:

Beautiful woman

Orchestrating her

Strategy for

Success

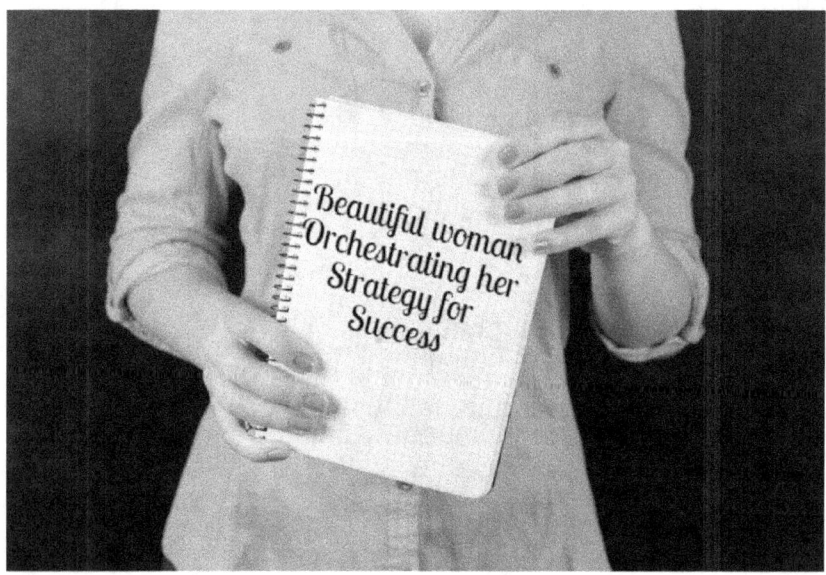

Nothing should hold you back from delving into the uncertain waters of entrepreneurship. You weren't placed on this earth to die without pursuing your passion. Allow that idea that has been in your mind to burgeon into a company that can change the world. Believe that you can accomplish this dream of creating a business, and you will put in the hard work to make it happen.

Entrepreneurship is a challenging, but exciting, journey. Alarming statistics about the failure rate of businesses may be encouraging you to crawl underneath a rock and bury your idea. The media proliferates the fact that close to 50 percent of businesses fail after the first 5 years. Fear of being a part of that statistic may be what is holding you back. Instead of focusing on the possibility of failure, focus instead on how you can be a part of the 33 percent of businesses that last for 10 years or more.

This book has been created to take you on the journey of business success from inception. We've not only shown you how to create your business, but how to ensure that it succeeds in the long-term. Useful tips and case studies are presented that can help you reap great success. Each step of creating a business is explained in ways that are simple to understand. We want this book to be your guide for entrepreneurial success. The onus is on you to carefully apply the strategies presented in this book so that the likelihood of success increases.

This book is written for women by women. We understand the challenges women face in a male-dominated world. Despite these challenges, always remember that you are a B-O-S-S. Let this book help you become a force to be reckoned with.

Happy reading!

Chapter 1
Understand World for Female Entrepreneurship

"A successful woman is one who can build a firm foundation with the bricks others have thrown at her."

James Brown, iconic soul singer, created a popular song in 1966 entitled *It's a Man's World.* That song has a powerful message that often rings true today. He vehemently states that it's a man's world because men have been the greatest inventors and were traditionally expected to be the providers of the household. However, he did admit that a man is nothing without a woman. Although this song relegates a woman to a supporting role in the grand-scheme of life, it underscores the value women add to the world.

More women began actively assuming more prominent roles in the 21st century. Women, such as Oprah Winfrey and Sheryl Sandberg, have proven that we can be a force to be reckoned with. We are now more empowered, independent, and ready to take on the world. We're here to kick a** and show men that we can be equal partners in running the world.

Sadly, the stereotype portrayed in James Brown's song is still prevalent today. Women are still trying to prove their worth in this male-dominated world where men still earn more than women in comparable jobs, and more opportunities are presented to male entrepreneurs than to female entrepreneurs. Gender inequality is still rife. Any woman who reads this book has to understand the dynamics of the business world from a female's perspective before even beginning to pave the path for her own business.

This chapter presents 2 case studies of female entrepreneurs who have worked assiduously to make their mark in their niches. Pay attention to the lessons from each story. Keep them in your thoughts as you begin to frame what you want your business to look like.

Patrice Banks, Founder of Girls Auto Clinic

Patrice Banks has disrupted the American auto-repair industry. In January 2017, she opened the first all-female all-in-one auto repair shop in America. Girl's Auto Clinic is the place where women can get full mechanic services from female mechanics, participate in apprenticeships if they're interested in the auto tech field, and get their hair and nails done at the Clutch Beauty Bar.

Her Challenges

Banks was a typical woman who knows very little about cars. She just drove them and wasn't overly concerned about keeping them well-maintained. One day, out of curiosity, she decided to perform a Google search to find female mechanics in her area. Surprisingly, none existed. That's when the idea hit...she needed to create a space where women could speak to other women about their car issues; women who would be patient and understand their needs.

Therefore, she started attending night classes to learn more about vehicles. She attended school while still working at her corporate job. Attending these classes showed her the first obstacle she had to face. She was the only female and, therefore, often felt intimidated. How could she measure up in a field that seemed so natural to men? Why should women trust her skills in a field meant for men?

She didn't let her fear deter her. She completed the program and was then faced with her next challenge. She was offered a job at a mechanic's shop that would pay $600 per week, a far cry from the cushy corporate job with a high salary. She had a tough decision to make. However, she believed in the potential of her idea and was determined to make it real. So, she accepted the job offer and spent the next 3 years honing her skills.

The glorious day came in January 2017 when she was able to open the doors of Girls Auto Clinic. Banks knew that she wanted to create a place where women wouldn't be taken advantage of because of their lack of knowledge about cars. Girls Auto Clinic, coupled with her workshops and self-published e-book *The Girls Auto Clinic Glove Box Guide*, is here to stay and make strides in helping women build confidence in maintaining their vehicles.

The Lessons

1. Banks took a giant leap of faith to enter an industry that very few women have even considered entering. She chose to break down gender stereotypes instead of uphold them. This shows that you can accomplish great things in any field, regardless of your gender. It's your commitment, stick-to-itiveness, and hard work that will help you realize success.

2. Knowledge and experience are crucial. You have to be willing to invest both time and money to gain the right knowledge and experience in your industry. Both investments can open opportunities that you may have otherwise missed. Banks willingly left her corporate job to work for a much lower salary so that she could gain valuable experience. She didn't dive in head-on.

3. Be passionate about your business. Banks had a strong conviction and knew that her vision could become reality. The market was there, ready for the taking. She took the leap of faith and her passion has kept her going.

9

Kerryanne Croft, Founder of the Vitamin M Box

Kerryanne Croft has always had a passion for business and people of color. Her creative flair, and desire to garner greater support for black-owned businesses, resulted in the creation of the Vitamin M Box. The Vitamin M Box is a subscription service that allows subscribers to get samples of products from businesses owned by black people.

The company is still in its early stages since it was established in May 2017. Thankfully, Kerryanne has been pleasantly surprised that her business has been receiving overwhelming support. The support has been so great that she is now considering securing financial backing since the business has been run so far using her finances. She notes that African-American women are the fastest growing group of entrepreneurs in America and hopes that she can continue to be a part of the growing movement. Her advice to you is: do the necessary research before diving in, plan ahead, and don't allow fear to stop you.

The Lessons

1. There is a growing support network for women in business since more women are becoming entrepreneurs. Now is probably the best time to begin your entrepreneurship journey.
2. Turn your passion into a business. Kerryanne's passion for uplifting the black community in America is what fuelled the creation of the Vitamin M Box.
3. Know your market and competitors before starting your business. Effective research and strategic planning are often what separate the winners from the losers.

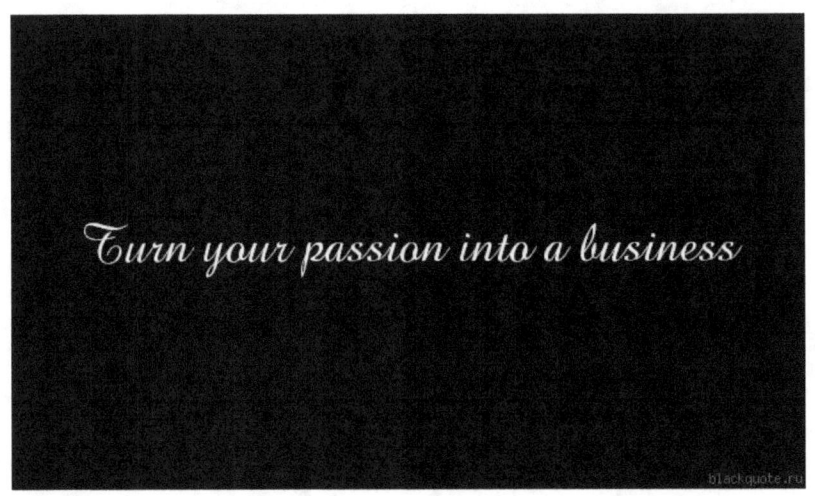

Turn your passion into a business

Some Additional Points

1. **Be true to who you are.** Don't think that you have to behave a certain way in a male-dominated space in order to be heard. Speak up so that you are heard, but let your genuine spirit and confidence shine through.

2. Few venture capitalist firms have female CEOs or board members. The likelihood of a female-owned business getting an investment increases when the potential investor is also a female. However, this shouldn't deter you from attempting to get capital from male investors. The aim of your pitch should be to show how an investor can get maximum return on his or her investment. Prove this and you'll have investors knocking at your door.

3. Dispel negative self-talk. There will be men who think you have no voice and should stick to what women should do. Don't listen to them and don't allow them to get into your head. Join a female entrepreneur support group so that you can hear some positive voices in your head.

4. Ensure that you have a good support system to assist with household and motherly duties.

Chapter One Action Item

Identify and join a female entrepreneur support group in your area.

Chapter 2
Identify a Suitable Business for a B-O-S-S Woman

"To succeed, you have to believe in something with such a passion that it becomes a reality."

~Anita Roddick

Businesses serve one core function: meeting the present and future needs of consumers. Entrepreneurs quickly learn how to make their brands believable and fully equipped to serve the needs of a market. Consumers, however, are often clearly able to identify companies that don't have an authentic identity...brands that are difficult to relate to. You can only truly be a B-O-S-S if you create a business that you're truly passionate about. Passion, essentially, is a part of the foundation that helps you build a solid business.

Therefore, before starting a business you must identify your passion. What makes your heart sing? What needs are you trying to address that you're truly passionate about? We are by no means suggesting that you should acquiesce to pursuing a passion that isn't profitable. However, you shouldn't make earning millions your primary objective. If you do, you'll more easily throw in the towel when the road gets rocky.

Marc Anthony has a clichéd saying that is often used when discussing careers and entrepreneurship. It says, "If you do what you love, you'll never work a day in your life." The trick is to find what you truly love. This chapter focuses on helping you identify your why...your true calling that can help you segue into a successful business.

Identifying Your Why

The previous chapter focused on the realities of business from a female's perspective. Creating that image in your mind was important to help you begin laying the foundation for your business. Kerryanne and Patrice clearly identified the reasons for creating their businesses. Both of their reasons stemmed from a genuine interest in their niches and true passion. Now, you need to identify the interests and passions you possess that can be used to create a business. These interests and passions are what will keep you going even when obstacles arise.

<u>Activity One</u>

1. State your primary interest; the thing that you enjoy that makes you want to get out of bed and face the day. Write this interest in the central circle.
2. State the skills you possess that are directly related to this primary interest. Write these skills in the outer circles.
3. List skills you are missing and educational resources that you can use for further training in the box located on the right.

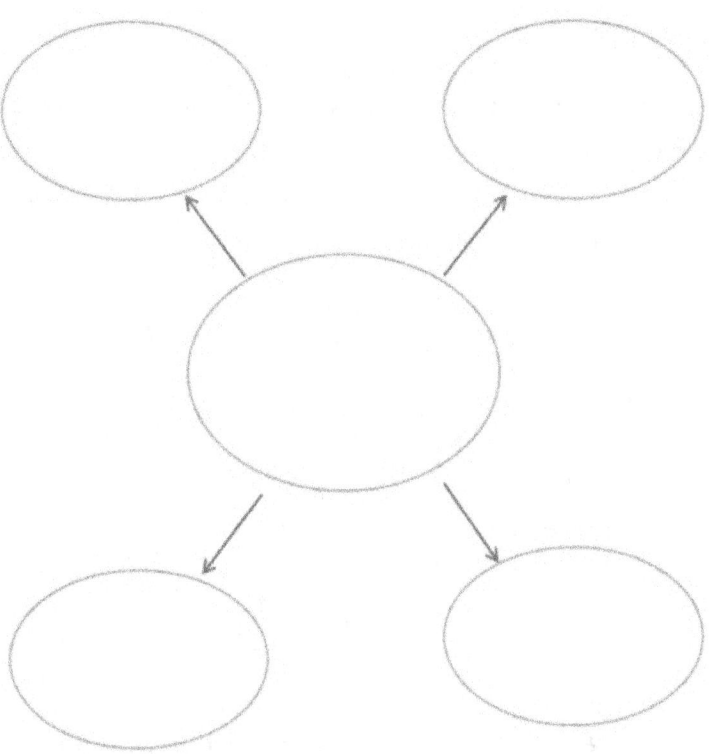

Missing Skills

Possible Sources for Further Education

Activity Two

List 2 or 3 unique perspectives that you can bring to the interest you have outlined. What can you bring to the niche that is new and fresh? What are the areas in which companies in your niche are lacking that you feel you can address?

Activity Three

Create a goal for your business based on the ideas you've written down for activity two. For instance, your passion may be beauty products. You may have realized that beauty vloggers tend to neglect women who don't like wearing makeup and live in developing countries. Your business goal could be...

"I am going to create a beauty vlog and website that makes any woman from the Caribbean feel like she can master simple makeup techniques. This vlog and website will feature products either made by Caribbean people or that can be easily sourced in Caribbean markets."

Attributes of a Female Entrepreneur

Always remember that a successful female entrepreneur is a B-O-S-S. You must, therefore, possess certain characteristics that help her make unbeatable strides. Successful women don't just get up one day and start chanting Beyoncé's "Who Run the World" anthem without having the characteristics listed below to support their confidence.

A Clear Vision

A female entrepreneur has to be able to see the big picture. Oftentimes, the big picture is not the most common opinion. You have to be ready to stand your ground and look for long-term gains instead of short-term pleasures. A true B-O-S-S revolutionizes her industry and inspires others to follow her lead. You can't achieve this without a clear vision of what you're hoping to achieve with your company.

Hard Work

Achieving greatness often takes time and hard work. All entrepreneurs have to be willing to put in the work to make their businesses successful. The hustle never ends.

Fearlessness

Successful women have the heart of a lion, but the spirit of a lamb. They know how to have the courage to be fierce while carrying the finesse that only a woman possesses. This doesn't mean that fear doesn't exist. However, a B-O-S-S woman knows how to transform that fear into fearlessness. You have to embrace this truth if you want to achieve success.

The Ability to Innovate

You're here to set trends, not follow them. You have to be able to see what the next big thing is going to be so that you can keep your business current and marketable. Always try to logically reinvent the wheel.

Innovation also means avoiding doing things just because everyone else is doing. Anything you decide to take on for your business must make sense for where your business is now and where you're hoping it will get to.

Flexibility

Female entrepreneurs quickly learn how to become juggle masters. You have to be able to juggle several things in one day while being flexible enough to handle unexpected changes. You'll often have to take a few minutes to readjust and approach a challenge from a fresh perspective. We don't live in a utopian society; unexpected things will happen and you have to be able to adjust.

Lifelong Learner

Entrepreneurs with an "I know it all" attitude tend not to get very far in business. Success comes to those who are willing to learn. You must use both your failures and successes as learning experiences. You must also be willing to constantly seek knowledge. Customers respect entrepreneurs who know what they're doing and can be viewed as experts in their niches. Constantly feeding your curiosity can keep you ahead of your competitors.

Taking Risks

You have to be willing to put yourself out there...to make your voice heard. This means stepping out of your comfort zone. You won't know what you can achieve until you take that leap of faith.

Positive Energy

Allowing negative energy to enter your physical and mental space leads to disaster. It's difficult to be positive all the time, especially when life doesn't seem to be working out the way you'd like. However, making a conscious decision to look for the positive in every situation and exude positive energy can help you earn the respect of those around you. People gravitate towards others who have a positive aura.

The Ability to Learn from Criticism

People will always have an opinion about your business and life. As a B-O-S-S entrepreneur, you have to listen to and learn from both positive and negative criticism. View criticism as opportunities for improvement rather than personal attacks. If there is nothing to be learned from the criticism, let it go. There is no need to hold on to toxic thoughts.

Integrity

A person who stands for nothing is like a leaf that floats in the air. It moves in whatever direction the wind takes it. Integrity is an important life skill. You have to know what you stand for and what you won't compromise on as a female entrepreneur. Compromising your values and being dishonest will come back to haunt you even if those actions provide temporary success.

Gratitude

Don't be overwhelmed by greed and power. Always remember the people who have helped you along the way. Be content with what you have and what you've already accomplished. The happiest people are the ones who rid themselves of envy. Stay in your own lane and remain thankful every day.

Conducting Market Research

You clearly outlined your passion and associated skills earlier in this chapter. You also focused on creating a goal that turns your passion into a potential business. This section focuses on determining the viability of your business.

Market research focuses on three key areas of business success: competitors, target demographic, and demand for product or service. It can be classified into 6 broad categories: secondary research, questionnaires, focus groups, interviews, or trials. Effective market research utilizes a combination of these categories so that enough information can be garnered about the 3 key areas of business success.

Identifying Your Competitors

Secondary research can be used to help you identify your competitors. Information can be obtained through internet research on reputable websites such as The New York Times, The

Economist, The Huffington Post, or even a simple Google search. Information can also be obtained from each company's social media pages. The following questions can be used to guide you through the research process:

1. Is there a company that is already providing what you have to offer? List all of these companies if there are multiple.
2. How long have these companies been in business?
3. What makes each of these companies unique? What are their strengths?
4. What do customers like about these companies?
5. What do you offer that is unique and better than what these other companies have to offer?

Target Demographic

It's important for you to be specific about the people you're hoping to target. Characteristics such as age, gender, location, income level, interests and even ethnicity should be considered. Research about your target demographic can also be done using secondary research. It's important for you to pay attention to how your target demographic changes. Your aim should be to meet the complex and changing needs of your audience.

The following questions can help you create a clear picture about your target audience:

1. Who are the types of people who would buy your products or services? What's unique about them?
2. What drives these people to make decisions?
3. Do they really need what I have to offer?
4. Will it be easy for me to reach them with my brand's message?

5. What media can I use to reach this audience?
6. How can I maintain the interest of this audience?

Demand for Your Product or Service

Supply and demand are the driving forces of economics. Your business won't be profitable if there is no demand for what you have to offer. Questionnaires, focus groups, trials, and interviews are the best tools to use for researching the demand for your product or service. Using a combination of these strategies provides a better overall picture of the demand. The pros and cons of each of these data collection methods are highlighted in the table below.

Data Collection Method	Pro	Con
Questionnaire	-Affordable if online and mobile versions are used. -Capture a wide range of data. -Information can be gathered from a wide audience. -Online tools, such as Survey Anyplace, provide simple questionnaire interpretation tools.	-Respondents may be dishonest and may misinterpret questions. -Cannot capture emotional responses or nonverbal communication. -Questionnaires with too many open-ended questions are difficult to analyze. -Respondents may

	You don't need to have a background in statistics to effectively interpret a questionnaire. -Provides anonymity. -You can ask as many questions as you desire.	be biased based on their perceptions about the product or topic. -Questions are more likely to be skipped if they are long or complicated.
Focus Group	-Participants' reactions can be easily seen and interpreted. -Good for investigating how groups think about a particular topic. -Can be used as a follow-up to results identified on questionnaires or through product	-Expensive because each participant is usually paid. -Moderators can influence participants' responses by directing the discussion based on their personal views. -Participants may not express their honest opinions

	testing. -Less time consuming than one-on-one interviews. -Respondents can seek clarification about questions they don't understand.	because of social pressure to provide what is deemed to be an appropriate response. -Can't cover as much as other forms of data collection.
Trials/ Market Testing	-Provides real data about the possible success of a product since the product is being offered to a real market. -A good way to test the market environment.	-One of the most expensive forms of market research. -Time-consuming. -It takes longer to get results than other forms of data collection.
Interviews	-Respondents can be accurately pre-screened. -Non-verbal communication can be identified.	-Costs are greater than those of a questionnaire. -The interviewer's ability to ask the right questions affects the quality of

		the responses.
		-An interviewer's bias can affect the line of questioning and, ultimately, the participant's responses.
		-Data entry will be tedious.
		-Sample size is greatly reduced.

Market research can help you save time and money. The results from the data collected allow you to determine if there really is a place for your product or service in the market. A combination of data collection strategies should be used to ensure that you get a very clear picture about the characteristics of your target audience and how your product or service meets their needs.

Chapter Two Activity

1. List the attributes of a female entrepreneur that you possess.
2. List the attributes of a female entrepreneur that you need to work on. Explain what you can do to develop these attributes.

3. Explain your target audience. For instance, a possible target audience for the beauty vlog mentioned in chapter one could be "Black Caribbean women between 18 and 30 years who are inexperienced with makeup application and want to learn the basic makeup techniques."
4. What did you learn about your competitors through your research? What are their strengths and weaknesses?
5. Follow these steps for creating an effective market research strategy

   a. Tick the data collection strategies that you can use.

	Questionnaire
	Focus Group
	Market Testing
	Interviews

   b. Plan a budget for your market research strategy. Only complete the areas that apply.

	Budgeted Amount	Actual Amount
Questionnaire creation software		
Questionnaire analysis software		
Data entry clerk		
Focus group participants		
Interview participants		
Interviewers/Moderators		
Manufacturing sample products for market testing		
Transportation		
Miscellaneous		

c. Write the steps for your market research strategy below. How long will it be done? How much data do you need for each strategy used? Who do you need to participate? How will you disseminate the information and organize focus groups or interviews? How will you compile the data? Where do you need to go for market testing, interviews or focus groups?

Chapter 3
Develop Your Brand

"When it comes to developing your brand, the first thing you need to know is yourself. Authenticity is what will drive you forward."

Who are you? On the surface, this seems like a very simple question to answer. Your first instinct is to probably state your name, profession, and place of residence. But, that question has much deeper meaning. It speaks to the core of your existence and is probing to discover what truly exists beyond the surface. This is your personal brand. It incorporates people's perceptions of you and the ways in which your core values and beliefs shape who you are.

Your business has its own personal brand. This chapter will help you clearly define your brand from what people see on the surface to the core beliefs that influence how it functions. There are aspects of brand development that will require input from your target audience. Therefore, some of the market research strategies outlined in chapter two will become useful.

Choosing a Name

A name is an identifying feature. It has to grab someone's attention, indicate the uniqueness of the product or service you offer and provide some connection to the product or service you're selling. The naming process for a business can be a tricky process. However, the following steps can help you choose a name for your business that can work with any marketing strategy.

Step One: Decide the message you want your business' name to convey.

You want to adequately convey what your business is about. Additionally, you want to create a name that will resonate with your target audience. A name that clearly identifies what your business doesn't need to be explained as much as one that doesn't. For instance, Juju Work wouldn't be the best name for a graphic design firm when compared with Juju's Graphic Designs. The latter explicitly states what the company offers.

Step Two: Be creative.

Think about using a new variation of an existing word. Combining variations of two words is also a possibility. Netflix is a good example of creative word combinations. Net is a shortened version of internet and flix is a variation of the word "flick" which is often used to represent a movie or film. Putting the two words together describes a company that allows users to watch "flicks" using the internet. Pretty neat huh?

Try to come up with at least 5 workable variations of possible company names. The more variations you have, the more options you can present during the testing stage.

Step Three: Run a test.

You need to determine if the names you've chosen are already being used. A simple trademark search using the USPTO Trademark Search System can help you do this. Tick off the names that pass the search.

It would be a good idea to create a focus group or an online survey requesting opinions about the names you've chosen. This is best done when you have also created the logo and slogan for your brand so that you can get their opinions about all of these elements at once.

You have to be very careful, however, about the persons to whom you send the survey. Remember that your target audience's opinion matters the most. Twitter has an interesting tool that allows you to post polls to your followers to gain opinions about various topics. You could consider creating a similar poll and running a Twitter ad targeted for your audience to get feedback. The option with the most votes would be the winning name.

Developing a Logo

Some of the most creative logos are simplistic in design, but have hidden meanings. Consider Amazon and Apple's iconic logos. Amazon's logo is just the company's name with an arrow connecting the first a to the z. That arrow indicates that Amazon offers all types of products ranging from a to z. the shape created by the arrow represents the fact that Amazon sells these products with a smile...a true commitment to customer service.

Apple's logo seems insignificant at first glance. In fact, the company's name seems like the strangest word for a company that sells technology products. Apple's logo designer realized that the word "bite" is an antonym for a computer "byte". So, he created a logo with a piece of an apple bitten off to portray this hidden message while representing the company's name.

Good and effective logo design takes time. Investing in a good graphic designer is important because you want to create a timeless logo that truly depicts the message of your brand. The following tips can help you work with your graphic designer to create the right logo.

- Look at the logos of your competition to see if you can identify any trends. There may be a common thread that ties companies in the niche together.
- Think about the personality of your brand. How can this personality be portrayed in the logo?
- Always remember that the logo is not always necessarily a potential customer's first point of contact with your brand. It should be considered an element of your overall brand image.
- Use clear typography that can make an impact at various distances. Remember that your logo will be used in all aspects of your brand. Business signage in once such area. Therefore, typography needs to be bold and clear so that a potential customer can see your company's name while driving along the road.
- Utilize negative space. Negative space is the blank space between letters and images in a design. Creative use of negative space can convey subliminal messages.
- Use colors in the right combination.
- Have your designer create 2 or 3 options that you can show to business partners or friends and family to get opinions.
- Think about how your logo can be transformed into an animated logo for digital media.

Developing a Slogan

Branding has to be consistent. Your slogan, therefore, should be linked to your logo, brand name, and core values. It may seem difficult to create a short slogan that incorporates all of these elements. But, the following tips can help you create a slogan that really packs a punch.

- Make it short and specific.
- Portray your unique perspective and the most important benefits of what you offer.
- Ensure that it can stand the test of time. Things change constantly in various niches. Your slogan should be strong enough to still be relevant despite these changes.
- It should be relevant to your target audience.
- Multi-national companies should have slogans that can be translated into other languages, but still have the same meaning.
- Create about 2 or 3 slogans that you can get feedback on using a questionnaire or focus group.

Examples of strong slogans, and the reasons for their strong impact, are presented below.

Sealy

Slogan: *Like sleeping on a cloud.*

Sealy sells mattresses. They are best known for their Posturepedic mattresses that provide full body support and comfort. Their slogan checks off all of the aforementioned tips. It paints a clear picture of what a customer can expect when one of their mattresses is bought: superior comfort.

Wal-Mart

Slogan: *Save Money, Live Better.*

Wal-Mart is America's official megastore brand that sells everything a customer could ever need at affordable prices. Their slogan helps customers conjure an image of getting items that can help them live comfortable lives without having to overspend.

KFC

Slogan: *It's finger lickin' good.*

KFC's slogan has been timeless. Anyone who sees that slogan is expecting the food served at KFC to be delicious. KFC's promise to customers is great fast food that they will enjoy.

Identifying Core Values, Vision and Mission Statements

Core values are the map that will steer the course of your business. They will also help you craft strong vision and mission statements. These questions will help you create a list of strong core values:

1. What problem is your business trying to solve?
2. What promises can you commit to make to your customers?
3. What does your business strongly believe?
4. What are your business' perspectives on societal issues that relate to your niche?

Your answers to these 4 questions will help you create a list of about 5 to 10 core values. These values can be grouped into categories. For instance, a list of core values for a graphic design business could be:

1. We will always create high-quality graphics that meet our clients' needs and are delivered on time.

2. We will pay attention to our client's ideas and ensure that they are incorporated and enhanced in the designs we create.
3. We will listen to our clients and respond within 24 hours to their queries and concerns.
4. Our fundamental belief is that graphic design is an artistic expression of what makes each brand unique. We strive to create products that artistically capture the essence of a business.
5. We will use eco-friendly paper for our printed materials and perform as much of our communication and collaboration online as possible. This will be our contribution to protecting the environment.

Articulating your company's core values paves the way for creating a vision statement. A vision statement clearly states your company's mid-term and long-term goals in a succinct manner. The following tips can be used to help you create the best vision statement.

- It shouldn't be longer than 1 sentence.
- It should be specific to the unique perspectives your business offers.
- It should use simple language so that people both inside and outside the organization can understand.
- It should be realistic, something that you and your team can actually achieve.
- It should relate to what you want your business to look like in 5 or 10 ten years. This means that it should be consistently evaluated to reflect the growth of the company over time.

- It should relate to the values you want your team to embrace.

Examples of Vision Statements

- Apple: "To create high-quality, low-cost, easy-to-use products that incorporate high technology for the individual."
- Tesla: "To accelerate the world's transition to sustainable energy."
- Facebook: "To give people the power to share and make the world more open and connected."

A possible vision statement for the graphic design company based on the core values mentioned is: "To create innovative designs that give each brand a unique voice."

> Branding has to be consistent. Your slogan, therefore, should be linked to your logo, brand name, and core values

Contrastingly, a mission statement is more specific than a vision statement. It gives an overview of how the vision will be realized and the time frame in which it will be realized. Additionally, it states typically states the target audience and provides direction for the organization. Your mission statement may change over time as your business grows and specific goals are accomplished. A possible mission statement for the graphic design company is stated below.

Juju's Graphic Designs is an online-based business focusing on artistic expressions that give a brand a voice. Each of our designers provides personalized attention and timely delivery that helps customers create unique branding elements for their businesses. We guarantee timeless designs, created using the most current and innovative technology, that depict the value of your brand.

This mission statement gives everyone at Juju's Graphic Designs a clear picture of their role in making the company succeed. They must provide personalized attention, meet deadlines, creative designs that can be used for the life of the business, and keep abreast of the newest and best technology to create and produce their designs. Customers also clearly see what the company offers.

Choosing the Right Location

Businesses have two options for modes of operation: online or from a store-front. Some businesses use a combination of both media. In fact, businesses that don't have an online presence tend to be less successful than others in this digital age. A store-front is necessary for certain types of businesses. The following tips should be adhered to if your business must operate from a storefront.

- Think carefully about your brand's personality. The physical location of your business should reflect this personality. An elegant restaurant, for instance, would need to be adorned with the right interior and exterior décor to reflect an image of elegance.

- Your storefront should be located in an area where your target demographic frequents. You don't want it to be in an area where it will go unnoticed. This may mean that you have to pay higher rental fees, but you want your business to thrive in the best area possible. Do our own observations to determine the amount of foot traffic in the area.
- There should be adequate parking and accessibility. Consider people with disabilities, traffic flow during peak hours, and the ease with which delivery trucks can deliver goods.
- Consider the opening hours of the facility if your business is located in an office building or shopping mall. Ensure that you can get access outside of office hours if you need to and that the heating and cooling systems are accessible.
- Proximity to your competitors is an important factor to consider. You may benefit from getting your competitor's overflow customers or customers who like to comparison shop. However, being too close to your competitor can be a marketing nightmare. Now your industry and competitors well to determine if close proximity will be an issue.
- Consider other businesses in the area, not just your competitors. Positioning is key. If you are positioned near a business in the area that gets high traffic, you can probably benefit from their foot traffic. This is especially true if you use geo-fencing strategies. Other businesses that are in close proximity can also provide services your employees will need. Such businesses include a daycare, gym, and places to eat.

- Choose the neighborhood carefully. Each neighborhood has its own image. For instance, a business in SoHo in New York would be perceived differently from a business in the Bronx. Also, research the success rate of previous tenants. Find out why previous tenants have had to leave.
- Check the zoning laws for the area. These laws could affect placing your business in the ideal location.
- Ensure that the building has the appropriate infrastructure to meet the growing demands of your modern business.
- Research rent, utility, and upfront fees.

Creating a 5 Year Plan

Your business is in its infancy so it may seem futile to create a 5 year plan when you don't even know how well the business will do in the next 6 months. Nevertheless, it's important to have a clear vision of how you want your business to grow over the next 5 years. Your vision has to be broken down into yearly goals and the resources needed to accomplish those goals.

An example of a possible 5 year plan for a restaurant is given below.

Year	Goal	Projected Profit***	Resources Needed
1	Open a location in downtown San Francisco that offers 6 specialty dinner dishes and	Break-even	-Top-range commercial appliances. -Well-trained staff

	begins to develop a reputation for creating quality food using local ingredients.		-Strong marketing strategy -Reliable local source for produce and meats
2	Expand the number of specialty dishes offered and include a live band.	$200,000	-Top-range commercial appliances. -Well-trained staff -Strong marketing strategy -Reliable local source for produce and meats Source for local live band talent.
3	Include a brunch menu and increase the seating	$300,000	-A large space. -Top-range commercial

	capacity.		appliances.
			-Well-trained staff
			-Strong marketing strategy
			-Reliable local source for produce and meats
4	Include a mini-coffee shop.	$500,000	-Reliable source for coffee beans.
			-Manager for the coffee shop.
			-A large space.
			-Top-range commercial appliances.
			-Well-

			trained staff
			-Strong marketing strategy
			-Reliable local source for produce and meats and coffee beans.
5	Open another location in San Francisco that follows the same model.	$1,000,000	-Capital to expand.
			-Manager.
			-Well-trained staff.
			-Top range commercial appliances
			-Strong marketing strategy

				-Reliable local source for produce, meats, and coffee beans.

*** Profit is not the same as revenue. A company can generate high revenue, but either breakeven be operating at a loss. Your profit is what is left after taxes, market value salaries, bills, and other commitments have been paid. Ensure that the projected profit is based on market information and realistic calculations. The numbers provided here are arbitrary values.

Chapter Three Activity

1. Develop a questionnaire or focus group interview questions that have your options for a business name and slogan. Carefully disseminate these instruments to the right people so that you can get useful feedback.
2. Visit UpWork, Fiverr, 99designs, or designcrowd to find an affordable graphic designer to develop the creative elements of your brand's image (the logo, letterhead, signage etc.).You can also do a general Google search to find a graphic designer in your area. Just type "Graphic designer in [insert location]."
3. Write your business' core values, mission, and vision statements.

4. Identify possible locations for your business if you're planning to have a storefront.
5. Create a 5 year plan for your business based on research.

Chapter 4
Understand U.S. Regulations for Businesses

"Every successful person in life began by pursuing a passion, usually against all odds."

Kim Kiyosaki

Moving forward with your business requires strict adherence to legal requirements. Legal requirements for small businesses vary from one state to another and heavily depend on the structure of the business. Fulfilling your legal responsibilities as a business owner is just as important as oiling the other moving parts that keep your business running. It's best to invest in a legal consultant who can help you get all of the legal requirements right at the early stages of your business. Looking for a cheap way out can result in expensive consequences in the long-term.

Types of Business Structures

Entrepreneurial novices tend to think that there are 3 types of businesses: small, medium, and large. That's true on the surface, but there are legal business structures that affect such things as the tax bracket in which your business falls and who is liable for the debt the business incurs. There are 6 types of business structures: sole proprietorship, partnership, corporation, S corporation, limited liability company (LLC), and limited liability partnership (LLP).

Sole Proprietorship (Sole Trader)

In a sole proprietorship, only one person is identified as the owner of the business. This sole proprietor pays personal income tax on profits earned from the business' profits. It is one of the most common forms of business structures used because it is the least complicated to establish. Additionally, it allows the owner to create the business under his or her own name instead of as a separate trade name.

Pros	Cons
- The owner's personal taxes are linked to the company's taxes. This makes it easier to file taxes. - All the business' profits go directly to the owner. - Business earnings are only taxed once per year.	-A sole proprietorship cannot obtain capital funding. -Your personal finances are at risk since the business' finances and your fiancés are linked. For instance, your personal assets could be taken by a debt collector to fulfill your company's debt obligation.

Limited Liability Company (LLC)

Most small businesses are restructured to create LLCs as they grow. In an LLC, the company's owners are not personally liable for the company's debts or liabilities. This option shouldn't be considered, however, if you're hoping to publicly list your company in the long-term.

Pros	Cons
- Easier to establish than a	- Death or

corporation. - Multiple owners are allowed. - The company's profits are a part of the owners' tax return. - Numerous shareholders are allowed.	bankruptcy of one owner means that the LLC has to be dissolved and restructured. It also has to be dissolved if a member retires or quits.

Limited Liability Partnership (LLP)

An LLP has a similar structure to a general partnership. However, it protects each member of the partnership by ensuring that each partner is only liable for his or her legal issues. It also provides the primary benefit of an LLC where each member is only liable for his or her own actions that bring the company into disrepute or debt. LLP's tend to be popular amongst lawyers and physicians.

Pros	Cons
- Allows a group of reputable professionals to pool resources and work together. Partners in a law firm, for instance, often have years of experience and come together so that they can share employees, office space,	- Some states view LLPs as non-partnerships for tax purposes. - Not all states recognize LLPs as legal business structures. - Only physicians and lawyers can form

and clients. This helps them reduce overhead costs.	LLPs in some states.
- Partners can be added or removed based on the conditions of the partnership agreement.	- Decision-making processes must be clearly outlined in a partnership agreement to avoid partners making crucial decisions on their own that affect the company.
- Partners get untaxed profits from the business.	

Partnership

Partnerships are created when more than one person owns the business. A general partnership differs from the LLP because all partners are responsible for the company's debts and liabilities. What one partner does affects all of the other partners. Limited partnerships also have two types of partners: general and limited. Limited partners are "silent" partners; they only invest and don't deal with the day-to-day operations of the business.

Pros	Cons
- A partnership's income is nontaxable. All profits and losses are passed on to the partners. However, a tax return must be filed showing the income and loss of	- General partners must stand liability for the business' debts.
	- One partner's business decision affects all the partners in the business.

the business and each partner should report his or her share of income and loss.	- Require more legal and accounting services thus making them more expensive to establish.

Corporation

Unlike the other business structures mentioned above, a corporation is a separate entity from its owners. Corporations have shareholders who accept limited liability. So, the business' profits are shared amongst them but they are not individually responsible for the company's debts. The shareholders appoint a board of directors charged with the responsibility of managing the daily operations of the company.

Pros	Cons
- The company's owner is not liable for any debt the company incurs. - Some profits are nontaxable. - Capital can be raised. The most common way to raise funds is through selling stocks. - Doesn't have to be restructured if something happens to one shareholder.	- More expensive to set up and maintain. - Governed by more rules which differ from one state to the next. - The corporation must pay federal and state taxes and taxes on the dividends issued to shareholders.

Subchapter Corporation (S Corporation)

An S Corporation merges the benefits of a partnership and a corporation. Owners of an S Corporation enjoy the perks of the structure of a corporation as an entity separate from the owner and avoid double taxation.

Pros	Cons
- Employees can be listed as shareholders and be paid tax-free dividends. - There is only one level of federal tax to pay. - The structure can be readjusted without exorbitant tax costs. - Greater opportunity for investors since an S Corporation can have up to 100 shareholders.	- Greater scrutiny from the IRS. - Expensive to establish. - Only one type of stock can be issued. This stock can only be owned by individuals, estates, and trusts outlined by the IRS.

Registering the Business

There are 4 general steps for registering your business regardless of the state in which the business operates. Each step is outlined below.

1. Register your business' name.

Your business won't be recognized as a legal entity until its name is registered. There are 3 steps to register a business name:

- Filing a "Doing Business As" (Fictitious Business Name). A DBA allows business owners to operate a business using a name other than their own. You file for a DBA at a local or county agency and pay a filing fee. Filing with a state agency, and publishing the name in a local newspaper as public notice, may also be required.
- Register an official business structure that gives you state protection.
- Trademark the name with the US Patent and Trademark Office. This gives you an added level of protection. The registration fee ranges from $275 to $325. More information can be found on the office's website www.uspto.gov.

2. Get your Employer Identification Number (EIN). Your EIN is also known as your federal tax ID. Also, check with your state agency to determine if you need a state number or charter.

3. Register with your state revenue agency to get your tax ID. This tax ID enables you to pay state, local, income, employment, and sales taxes.

4. Acquire licenses and permits. Licenses and permits differ from one type of business to the next. Speak with a legal advisor or your state agency to get more information.

Understanding IRS Requirements

Tax evasion and tax fraud are serious crimes. Paying copious amounts of money from your business to the IRS may make your heart cringe. But, those tax dollars are what help America thrive. Don't be tempted to create offshore accounts and alter your books to reduce the amount you pay in taxes. Also, don't allow ignorance to create problems between you and the IRS. Speak with an accounting professional to ensure that you correctly file all of the IRS and state tax forms required for your business structure.

Chapter Four Activity

1. Hire a legal consultant and accountant to help you with the legal aspects of formally establishing your business.
2. Choose the best business structure for the type of business you want to create.

Chapter 5
Learn to Lead

"If your actions inspire others to dream more, do more and become more, you are a leader"

John Quincy Adams

Leaders lead. Full stop. Entrepreneurs always have a team of people who keep the wheels of their business turning. Although you are a B-O-S-S female entrepreneur, you also have to know how to lead your team to greatness. A leader who leads knows how to inspire his or her team to embrace the vision instead of dictate results. Excellent leaders know how to inspire greatness, not fear. It doesn't matter how much you believe in your vision, your team must believe in it as well and believe in you. Otherwise, your business will slowly fall apart.

Attributes of an Effective Leader

An effective leader is not a manager. Inspiration forms the core of everything a leader does. A leader's job is to help each team member give the best talents and skills that propel the company forward. Some of the attributes that a leader must possess in order to do this are outlined below.

Good Communicator

Communication is a two-way process. We must both send and receive a message, paying attention to verbal and non-verbal cues. Effective leaders don't sit behind their desks and communicate with their team members solely via email. This approach is impersonal and is often met with a lack of response and action.

Effective leaders take the time to speak with their teams face-to-face. They actively listen to what each person has to say. Active listening is about giving the person speaking your full attention without thinking about the next thing that you want to say. It requires you to make an effort to rephrase what the person has said to ensure that you've understood the message. It also requires paying attention to the non-verbal cues that may be presenting a hidden message. The person speaking should feel like his or her concerns and opinions matter.

When a leader speaks, everyone willingly listens. The message is also clearly presented so that there is no room for ambiguity. Confidence and clarity of written and spoken word are paramount.

<u>Willing to Learn</u>

An effective leader understands that he or she doesn't know it all. Experience can teach wisdom, but it can also prevent you from keeping abreast with new and exciting trends. Create an environment when your team members feel like their ideas and concerns will be listened to and acted upon. Some ideas may be unrealistic; others may help you strike gold.

Additionally, a lot of criticism will be thrown your way. It makes no sense brooding over the words that are said and lamenting about how much you've done and how you disagree. Adopt a solution-oriented mindset by focusing on the constructive aspects of the criticism. What can you learn? How can you improve?

<u>Provides Useful Feedback</u>

Leaders receive criticism and issue criticism. Poor leaders demean their team members and provide feedback that is too ambiguous for them to learn from. A good leader knows how to communicate feedback in a positive way. Good feedback for an employee strikes a balance between that person's strengths and weaknesses. It shows that the leader sees the good work that is being done, but has identified some areas that need a bit of work.

Identifying the weakness is one thing. Helping the team member to work on it is another. Effective leaders provide the resources and support needed to help that team member transform weakness into a strength.

Invests in Team Members

Entrepreneurs sometimes think that it's pointless to invest in an employee because that money is "wasted" if the employee decides to leave. Effective leaders aren't afraid of their employees moving on to other opportunities. In fact, they encourage it. However, they ensure that they do all they can to help each employee function effectively in their jobs. This means providing training opportunities, promotions, and tasks that appropriately challenge the employee. A leader is always excited about an employee's growth and what that growth means for the business' success.

Treats Team Members as Humans, not Robots

Effective leaders take the time to get to know each employee. All employees from the janitor to a senior level executive are important. People are more loyal and willing to contribute to the success of a company that cares about them. Leaders should encourage team members to establish a work-life balance and be provided with the tools they need to be more productive at work. Overtime should be discouraged, but in the rare cases where it is necessary, it should be compensated.

Opportunities should also be provided for employees to have fun and bond. Team leaders should check up on their team members not just to find out if a job has to be completed, but also to find out how they're doing physically and emotionally. How's their family doing? Are there issues at home that could be compromising their ability to focus? Any emotional issues that are identified should result in a referral to a counselor. Promoting holistic wellness amongst staff is crucial.

Works with the Team

An effective leader understands that leading isn't about telling people what to do. It's about working with people to get things done. They aren't afraid to get down in the trenches, roll up their sleeves, and get to work. They know that leadership is more than just a position; it's a huge responsibility to influence others. They don't stand at the front and dictate, but they sit with their team and work with them to face each challenge along the way.

Makes Decisions Based on Facts not Emotions

There is a common picture painting of women that portrays us as weak and poor decision makers. Women are thought to make decisions primarily based on emotions instead of examining the facts. Female entrepreneurs must separate emotions from facts in decision-making.

Trust their Team Members

Effective leaders know that they have a team for a reason. They don't try to take every task upon themselves and micromanage. Instead, they trust the creativity and skills of their team members. They delegate tasks and have confidence that their team will get things done.

Displays Integrity and Honesty

Effective leaders always stand for what is right, even when what is right isn't the popular opinion. Your team will lose respect for you if you're dishonest and willing to do anything, even the most unethical of things, just to make a buck. Good things follow those who live with integrity and honesty.

Displays Resilience

Effective leaders are stoic in the midst of a crisis. You have to see the problem and immediately begin devising a solution instead of plunging into despair. Catastrophe may be surrounding you, but you must be committed to finding the most ethical solution. Displaying this resolve is important for preventing your team from falling apart.

Tips for Motivating Your Team

A motivated team creates a successful company. Effective leaders create motivated teams by embracing the aforementioned attributes and following these useful tips.

- Pay team members at market value. Hiring a plethora of employees only to pay them menial salaries is futile. It's better to hire less staff, pay each person what they're worth, and distribute the work amongst them. Employees who are paid at or above more market value are more likely to be loyal to a company.

- Create a pleasant work environment. No one wants to work in an environment where a negative cloud seems to be permanently fixed. Pleasant work environments encourage people to want to get out of their beds and come to work more often than not.
- Provide opportunities to learn new skills and hone existing ones. This point was alluded to earlier. It's mentioned here because it is important. Investing in your employees pays in the long-term. It's better to have a team with strong skills who can face virtually any challenge unique to your business than to have one that struggles at every step. Paying consultants and outsourcing some services is far more expensive.
- Encourage collaboration. Employees need to feel that their voices are heard and their opinions are valued. They also need to be provided with the resources they need to work effectively.
- Use mistakes as learning opportunities. Failure is a part of life. How we deal with it is what determines future success. Don't punish team members for honest mistakes. Help them identify the lessons that can be learned from the experience so that they don't make the same mistake again.
- Ensure goals and expectations are clear. You can encourage your team leaders to set weekly goals with associated checklists for their respective teams. This helps all employees know what they should accomplish each week and how they'll know that the goal has been met.

- Only have meetings when absolutely necessary. Meetings waste time. Short meetings that are spaced out over a period of time are better than longer, frequent meetings. Get to the point quickly so that people have more time to complete action items arising from the meeting.
- Show appreciation to all team members. This could be in the form of an award ceremony or a simple thank you note. Just remember that it is important for all of your employees to feel appreciated.
- Allow team members to use their own unique strategies to solve problems. Everything doesn't have to be done your way. There is more opportunity for growth when creativity is encouraged.
- Give team members more opportunities to work in their areas of strength.
- Organize team-building activities. These activities help to encourage a positive team spirit.

Chapter Five Activity

1. Identify a female leader you admire. List the qualities about this person you admire and state why you admire these qualities.
2. List your strengths and weaknesses. How do you think your weaknesses will affect your ability to lead effectively? How can you address these issues?
3. Plan the organizational structure for your startup. Use this structure to determine the maximum number of employees you need to hire, the teams you'll need to have, and the team leaders.
4. Work with your team leaders to create realistic reward systems, awards, and team-building activities.
5. Plan training sessions for your team leaders and your entire staff.

Chapter 6
Networking to Make the Dream Work

"If you want to go fast, go alone. If you want to go far, go with others."

African Proverb

Entrepreneurship is often viewed as a sprint with each entrepreneur using every trick in the book to win the race. Healthy competition challenges businesses to become better. That fact can't be denied. However, an entrepreneur who tries to win the race alone is a fool. Entrepreneurship should be viewed as a hike up Mount Everest; a feat that is best undertaken using team rather than individual effort. An entrepreneur's team isn't limited to her employees. This dream team also includes a network of experts who form the bridge between the entrepreneur and crucial resources needed for the company to thrive.

Always remember that you can't embark on this entrepreneurial journey alone. Creating and searching for opportunities to forge connections with key players in your industry, as well as entrepreneurs from other industries, is vital to your business' success. Think about networking as an intricately woven spider's web. Each connection, each fiber strengthens the web. Similarly, the more meaningful connections you make, the stronger your business will become. This chapter provides some useful networking tips that will help you form the right connections.

Connecting with Other Entrepreneurs

Networking isn't restricted to people within your industry. All entrepreneurs experience common challenges and have invaluable insights to share. Building relationships with other entrepreneurs can help you:

1. Identify the best angel investors and venture capitalists to approach for funding.

2. Create partnerships with companies from other niches that can help reduce operating costs and boost productivity.

3. Develop a support system filled with people who have first-hand experience with what you're going through.

4. Gain inspiration through the passion other entrepreneurs exude.

5. Gain invaluable insight about how to overcome challenges you may be facing on your entrepreneurial journey. This point is particularly important because it helps you save both tie and money.

6. Benefit from business opportunities that may not have been otherwise accessible.

7. Increase your confidence as you learn to step out of your comfort zone.

8. Increase the visibility of your

Tips for Connecting with Other Entrepreneurs

1.   Become an active Twitter user.

Twitter provides a unique opportunity for entrepreneurs to find other entrepreneurs from around the world. Type #entrepreneur in the search engine and you'll be amazed by the stream of results that emerge. Check the Twitter profiles of the people who interest you. If they reply to posts that are directed at them, it's likely that they will respond to you.

You can also check out Twitter live chats within your niche or in other niches that interest you. Twitter live chats provide an interactive environment for engaging in dialogue about particular topics in real-time. The rules for participating are:

1.   Log on to Twitter at the time of the chat.

2.   Use the stated hashtag to engage in the discussion. Your comments won't be visible in the chat if you don't use the hashtag.

3.   Most chats follow a question and answer format. So, follow the questions being asked and answer accordingly.

4.   Follow the specific rules stipulated by the host of the Twitter live chat.

Some useful Twitter chats to engage in are:

-#SmallBizChat which is held on Wednesdays at 8 pm EST

-#PMChat which is held on Fridays at 12 pm EST

-#WorkTrends which is held on Wednesdays at 1:30 pm EST

Days and times of these chats may change. It's important to regularly check for any changes.

2. Join an entrepreneurial organization.

Entrepreneurial organizations bring entrepreneurs from a variety of niches together. Many of these organizations host networking events, training sessions, and provide opportunities for members to consult with each other. Some of the top organizations to join are:

- Entrepreneurs' Organization (EO)

- Young Entrepreneur Council (YEC)

- Founders card

- Social Enterprise Alliance (SEA)

- Startup Grind

- Edward Lowe Foundation (ELF)

- Vistage

- Association of Private Enterprise Education (APEE)

- Young Presidents' Organization (YPO)

- United States Association for Small Business and Entrepreneurship (USASBE)

- Ashoka

- The Entrepreneur's Club (TEC)

3. Plan your own local networking event.

Organizing a networking event isn't easy. However, there may not be any networking events in your area. This vacuum provides the perfect opportunity for you to step in and make a difference. A well-planned and well-executed event will help you earns the respect of your community and meet entrepreneurs you may not have known existed.

4. Work from a co-working space.

A co-working space provides numerous benefits for a solopreneur (an entrepreneur, typically a freelancer, with a small enough business to run it alone). Co-working spaces emerged over the past 5 years in response to the growth of the freelance industry. Freelancers needed a space to be productive, have meetings with clients, and collaborate with other freelancers. Co-working spaces solve these problems. Consider using a co-working space to meet other freelancers if you're in that industry.

5. Attend conferences.

The benefits of attending a conference are two-fold. You're able to learn more about recent developments in your industry while meeting other people who are interested in your niche. A Google search can help you find conferences in your area. For instance, if you want to find conferences in San Francisco related to blogging you would type "Blogging conferences in San Francisco 2017" in the search bar. You also have to determine if the cost to attend the conference is within your budget.

Tips for Making Connections at Networking Events

Attending a networking event is pointless if you don't make the right impression. You don't have to be loud or obnoxious to be noticed. These pointers will give you the power to make an impact.

-	Time is everything. Any conversation you have at a networking event gives you less than a minute to make a strong impact. You have 7 seconds to make the right first impression, 14 seconds to create intrigue, and 21 seconds to share the story behind your business. Practice with one of your closest friends and make changes based on the feedback provided.

-	Invest in well-made business cards. Business cards get your foot in the door and can be a talking piece if they are attractive. Consider metal business cards. Also, consider how you can adequately present what your business has to offer in less than 3 minutes.

-	Communication is a two-way street. It's easy to get caught up in the message you are trying to present instead of listening to the other person. Display genuine interest in what the other person has to say. Allow the person to speak.

-	Think about how you can create mutually beneficial relationships with the people you meet. Don't attend networking events with a selfish mindset; only being concerned about what you can get from the event. Instead, think about how you can help another entrepreneur just as much as that entrepreneur helps you. Win the person's trust before trying to sell yourself ice or product.

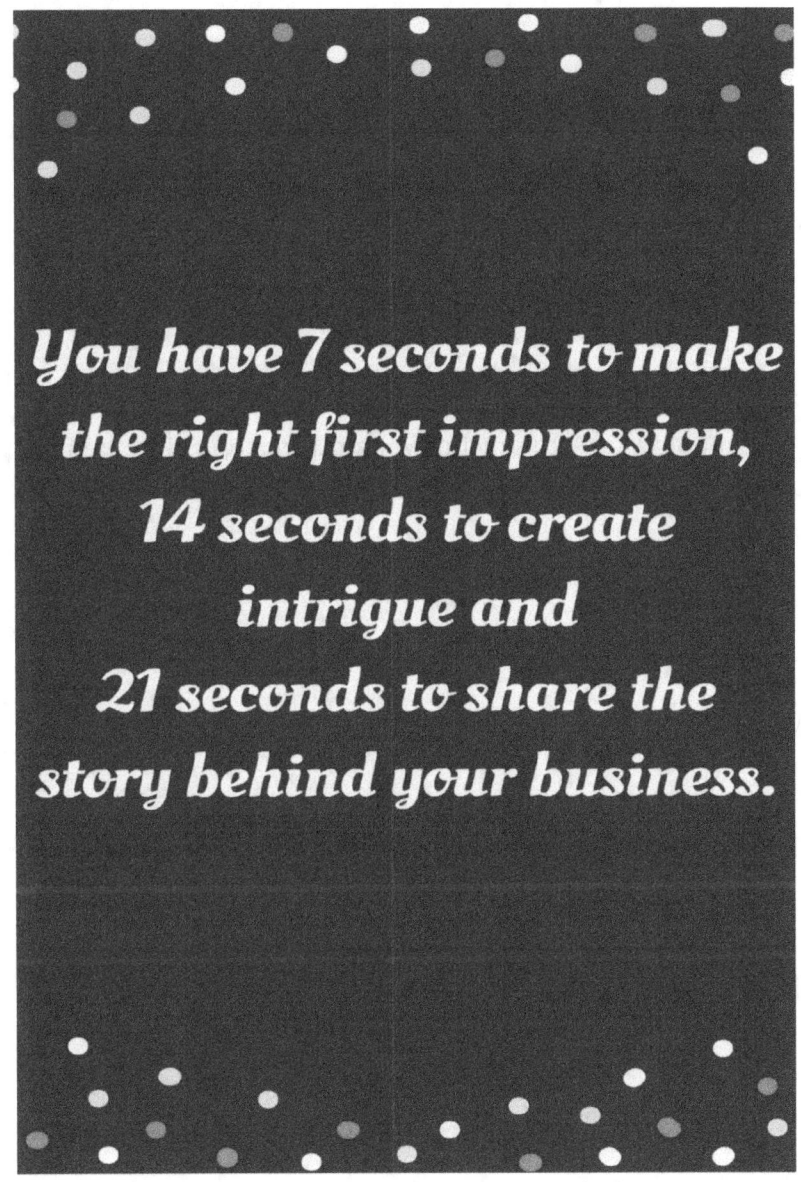

You have 7 seconds to make the right first impression, 14 seconds to create intrigue and 21 seconds to share the story behind your business.

- Don't delay follow-up contact with the people you meet. Making contact as soon as possible shows how committed you are to maintaining the connection.

Chapter 6 Activity

1. Make a list of possible networking activities you can attend this month.

2. Prepare business cards.

3. Describe your business in 3 sentences.

4. Schedule a time to practice your introductory statements.

Chapter 7
Get Money for the Piggy Bank

"When looking for funding, don't just look for cash. Look for the right people."

Jodie Fox

Successful startups have a strong foundation based on the PTC principle. The PTC principle states that passion, teamwork and cash-flow are essential elements of a successful business. The previous chapters covered passion and teamwork. Cash-flow is the focus of this chapter.

It is often recommended that outside investors shouldn't be acquired during the early stages of a startup. An entrepreneur would be relinquishing control of certain aspects of his or her company too soon. Other pitfalls of seeking investors too soon include:

- Investors have a vested interest in the business and will, therefore, demand to be a part of decision-making processes. Some investors can be good mentors; others can be predators who only offer negative criticism. Distinguishing between both can be difficult.
- Investors may take the company away from you.
- You could end up wasting money and time looking for the right investor and subsequently dealing with investor relations. Time and money are your most valuable assets, especially when you are just starting a company.
- Investors usually want you to work with a large, well-rounded team. A large team isn't beneficial for a startup

because of high salary fees and the need to re-train when a strategy has to be redirected. It's best to start with a small team and scale up as the business grows.

This presents a conundrum for a novice entrepreneur. How do you know the best time to seek investors for your company?

The Right Timing for Seeking Investors

The pitfalls previously outlined don't negate the fact that investor capital can help a company thrive. Timing, however, is pivotal in ensuring this happens. The following indicators should guide you in making the decision about the best time to search for investors.

Indicator #1: You Don't Need Capital

This may seem counterintuitive, but the best time to raise capital is actually when you don't need it. Your company is doing well and you know that the injection of capital will help it grow even faster. This doesn't mean that you'll enter a pitch and say, "I don't know what I need your money for. I just need it." Searching for an investor challenges you to look for growth opportunities. You'll become an innovator who stays ahead of the competition.

Indicator #2: The Market is Ripe

A downturn in the market can actually be a good time to seek investors. Your company should be in good financial standing, despite the downturn, so that it looks like a safe investment. You'll usually be able to get good investment rates in these downturns. This investment can be used to gain ground in your industry while others are scrambling to survive. The trick is to effectively lead your company and effectively manage funds so that the company won't be affected by a market downturn.

Indicator #3: You Have a Minimum Viable Product

Investors typically only invest in proven concepts. You can approach investors when you've tested your product on the market and have reached a point where the demand has outgrown your ability to supply. Investment capital is about helping your company move from one accomplishment to the next.

Indicator #4: You Have no Capital to Begin

All entrepreneurs would have enough money to get their businesses started in an ideal world. This isn't the reality for many entrepreneurs, especially those who have to manufacture products instead of sell services. Falling into this category means that you will have to seek early-stage funding. Pay attention to the following considerations when seeking early-stage funding:

1. Calculate the amount of working capital you will need to develop and launch the product within 18 months.
2. Give up as little equity as possible. You will need more equity for future funding rounds.
3. Calculate a reasonable valuation supported by evidence.

Seeking capital to start your company is strongly discouraged. Furthermore, the probability of investors only investing in the possibility of success is slim. Only resort to early-stage funding if you really have no savings that can be used to test your product on the market.

Bootstrapping, Borrowing or Seeking an Investor

You've decided that you need funding for your business. However, you are uncertain about the most appropriate method of funding to use. You have four choices: bootstrapping, borrowing, angel investors, or venture capitalists.

Bootstrapping

Think about bootstrapping like backpacking across a continent. A backpacker knows how to resourcefully use the funds and resources available to create a memorable trip. Entrepreneurs bootstrap by pooling funds in unconventional ways. Crowdfunding is one of the most popular forms of bootstrapping.

Crowdfunding allows people to volunteer to contribute any amount of money they desire to help develop your idea. In return, they can receive a prototype of your product or some other type of incentive. Kickstarter , Indiegogo, RocketHub, and GoFundMe are the most popular crowdfunding websites.

Founders of the Pebble wristwatch used crowdfunding to raise funds. The company began in 2012 and revolutionized the smart watch industry with its unique design. Within 2 hours of creating the campaign, the founders reached their $100,000 crowdfunding goal. They then raised $1 million in 28 hours and eventually raised $10 million. Their campaign is one of the most successful Kickstarter campaigns of all time. However, their exponential growth and fierce competitors eventually caught up with them. FitBit acquired Pebble in 2016. Nevertheless, their successful campaigns demonstrate that it is possible to get adequate funding if you have an idea that resonates with the market.

Borrowing

Borrowing can come in the form of bank loans or loans from family and friends. A well-written business plan should always be created before approaching a bank or an individual for a loan. Strategies for creating an effective business plan will be discussed later in this chapter. The business plan and a stellar pitch can help you convince lenders that your business will earn enough profit to sufficiently pay back the loan.

The beauty of a bank loan is that you don't have to relinquish business equity. The process for acquiring a bank loan can, however, be long and tedious. Loans from family and friends provide more flexible terms, but may require giving up some equity depending on the level of business savviness of the lender.

Angel Investors

An angel investor is an individual with a high net worth looking to invest in the next big thing. Although their money is an investment that doesn't have to be repaid, you do have to give up some amount of equity in your business. This, therefore, means that the angel investor will have some say in the decision-making processes of the business. Nevertheless, angel investors are more willing to take risks and invest thousands of dollars. You can find angel investors through the networks you created as a part of the previous chapter, or by visiting angel.co or angelcapitalassociation.org.

Venture Capitalists

Venture capitalists tend to be companies rather than individuals. Unlike angel investors, they usually don't take the risk of investing in the early stages of a startup. However, they tend to invest more capital than angel investors. Venture capitalists also take equity in your business and may even require a greater equity share than angel investors.

Creating an Effective Business Plan

A business plan outlines important facets of your business that can guide an investor's decision. It also provides you with a guide that can be used to gauge how well you're accomplishing your goals. Effective business plans have the following components:

1. Executive Summary
2. Business description
3. Sales and marketing
4. Operations
5. Management Team
6. Development (Future Growth)
7. Financial Summary

The Executive Summary

The executive summary is a synopsis of what is covered in the business plan. It shouldn't be more than one page long and should adequately describe the essential features of your company. Most potential investors don't have the time to sift through your entire business plan. Therefore, they may only focus on the executive summary.

Business Description

The business description is the section where you explain what makes your business unique, your vision and mission statements, goals, and anything that has contributed to the company's success thus far. It should provide a clear picture of how your business is strategically positioned against competitors.

Sales and Marketing

This section consists of:

1. A description of the niche in which your business operates
2. General costs (production or service costs for instance). More financial details are provided in the financial section of the business plan.
3. Customer acquisition strategies

Operations

The administrative details of your business are outlined in this section. It should include an outline of your organizational structure, the operational flow of the organization, the location of the office, network of suppliers, general operation expenses, and legal relationships.

Management Team

You work with a team of leaders who help the company run smoothly. This section allows you to list your advisers and team leaders and explain the value each person brings to the team.

Development (Future Growth)

Leaders are visionaries. Your business may be young, but you must already have a clear picture of how you want it to grow. Your plans for future growth should be detailed in this section. It should be well-researched and describe your goals and plans for the business.

Financial Summary

At the end of the day, the numbers are what matter. The financial summary should include the personal financial statement of each owner, balance sheet, income statement, and cash flow statement. There should also be a section for projecting future earnings based on present earnings.

Strategies for Creating a Winning Pitch

A business plan puts everything that makes your business uniquely positioned for success on paper. The pitch is essentially the verbal presentation of the business plan. The pitch is what really sells an investor on your business. There are 3 types of pitches: the elevator pitch, the short-form pitch, and the long-form pitch.

The Elevator Pitch

Think about the last time you traveled on an elevator. The elevator ride more than likely lasted less than 2 minutes. An elevator pitch is based on this concept; you have to pitch your business in less than 2 minutes. There's no time to delve into numerous details. You have to get to the point quickly and ensure that what you say makes an impact. An elevator pitch must include the problem that your business is trying to solve and how your business plans to solve that problem.

A good elevator pitch gets your foot in the door. It piques the interest of a potential investor who will feel compelled to call you for a follow-up meeting. It's highly unlikely that the investor will be saying, "That was great! Here's $100,000." after hearing your elevator pitch. They are going to want to learn more about your business to determine if it really is a viable investment.

The Short-Form Pitch

A short-form pitch usually lasts between 5 and 10 minutes. It should describe the problem you're trying to solve, how your company solves the problem, details about your niche, the team you work with, competitors, key financial details (such as profits earned in the past year), and goals for the future.

The Long-Form Pitch

Twenty minutes is the ideal length of a long-form pitch. Anything over that results in those listening losing interest. Your presentation should use a combination of audio-visual material and should also include testimonials from people who have used your products or services. It's important to use statements supported by facts instead of opinions. For instance, don't say "We sell the best beauty products in the industry." Say instead that "Our beauty products have been used by over 20,000 customers who have achieved amazing results."

Qualities of a Good Negotiator

Let's say that you impress the investor. The investor may want to present terms of the agreement or increase the equity stake. This may not be something you agree with. So, you have to put on your negotiator hat. A good negotiator:

- Expects the unexpected and knows how to adjust accordingly
- Researches the person with whom he or she is negotiating to understand the things that matter to this person.

- Goes into a negotiation with an idea of the least acceptable result (LAR), most acceptable result (MAR), and best alternative to a negotiated agreement (BATNA)
- Practices patience and creativity
- Actively listens
- Pays attention to both verbal and non-verbal cues
- Leaves emotions behind and doesn't take things personally
- Is flexible
- Works towards finding a mutually beneficial solution

Chapter 7 Activity

1. Do you need investment capital at this stage of your business? Explain your answer.
2. What type of funding source will you use to fund your business?
3. Create a business plan.
4. Write an elevator pitch, short-form pitch, and long-form pitch.

Chapter 8
Create a Digital Brand

"Reach, don't preach. Digital marketing is simply about putting your customer first."

Author Unknown

Strong brands create a ubiquitous online presence. Websites, social media platforms, and digital marketing initiatives open up a world of possibilities that help a brand truly stand out. A B.O.S.S. entrepreneur knows that there are 3 integral components of a strong digital brand:

1. An effective website
2. Engaging social media profiles
3. Content marketing

Entrepreneurs who expertly weave these components together are able to create a strong online presence. This chapter focuses on these 3 critical areas and how you can get them to work together seamlessly.

Tips for Creating an Effective Website

The growth of technology has increased consumers' expectations. The internet has become people's go-to for finding goods and services, shopping, interacting, dating and doing a myriad of other things that were traditionally done face-to-face. A company without a strong website is losing a large market of potential customers.

There are 4 types of business-related websites:

1. General business websites
2. E-commerce websites
3. Portfolio websites
4. Podcasting websites

General business websites can combine features of e-commerce, portfolio, and podcasting websites. Nevertheless, the type of website you use isn't as important as the features that make the website work. Effective websites are:

1) Search engine optimized
2) Relevant
3) User-friendly
4) Highly responsive
5) Able to load quickly
6) Secure
7) Mobile Friendly

Search Engine Optimization (SEO)

Potential customers often find websites by typing keywords into a search engine. If you want to find a nail salon in New York, for instance, you would type "nail salon New York", "nail salon in New York" or "New York nail salon". Including relevant keywords and keyword phrases on your website is one aspect of SEO. Some other key points to remember about keywords are:

- They should be location specific to better reach mobile users.
- Keywords associated with your services or blog topic should also be used. For instance, if you're writing content

about Thanksgiving recipes you should consider words such as turkey, cranberry sauce, and pumpkin.

- Longer content allows you to strategically include relevant keywords more effectively. This doesn't mean that long content of poor quality will hit the mark. Both length and quality work in tandem.

The trick with keywords, however, is that they have to be written as naturally flowing text. Keyword stuffing and misuse provides no benefit to the reader or content creator. In fact, Google frowns upon keyword stuffing. It's more prudent to write naturally rather than focus on inserting as many keywords as possible.

Additionally, the content of the website has to be relevant. For instance, a nail salon in New York shouldn't have content about bungee jumping. The content on this company's website should relate to aspects of the nail industry. Furthermore, content used in social media campaigns should relate to the content found on the website page to which the campaign is linked.

Link building is another important SEO strategy. Some people get very creative with link building by collaborating with blog writers to have a link to their website included in popular blog posts. Other areas where links to your website can be included are:

- A social media profile
- Submitting your website link to an online directory
- Paying for listings
- Blog comments (can be considered spam if overused so be careful)

A website should also be optimized for voice searches. The following strategies will help you create a voice search optimized website:

- Create a Google My Business listing
- Use conversational keywords. Think about how people talk and ask questions in real life. A FAQ page provides a good opportunity to use these long phrases and questions.
- Get structured data markup from schema.org

Short and relevant URLs perform better in search engine rankings. A URL with more than 5 words is less likely to receive the recognition it deserves. For instance, cemwritingservices.com is a good URL for a company that offers writing services.

Relevant

Websites should be relevant not only to boost SEO rankings but also to appeal to the intended audience. Clicking a URL for a website that we expect to be one thing but is something totally different is a complete turnoff. Websites that portray this image send the wrong message and lose potential customers fast. You can make your website relevant by:

- Understanding the characteristics and interests of your target audience. It's impossible to write content that interests everyone. However, you can write content that keeps your intended audience in mind.
- Paying attention to user intent. A user performs an internet search to perform a particular task (such as purchase clothing), gain new information or find locations. The user intent is what should inform the keyword research of your site.

- Writing compelling meta descriptors. Meta descriptors are code in the website's page header that shows in search engine results pages. The catchier they are, the greater the likelihood of someone clicking on the URL.
- Creating a relevant and catchy headline. The headline is the first thing a user sees when being directed to your homepage. Therefore, it needs to grab attention while remaining relevant.
- Having a blog component to your website that provides solutions to relevant problems.

User-Friendly

Simply put, a user-friendly website is easy to navigate. There are some websites that are more confusing thank helpful. A website can be made more user-friendly by:

- Lessening the number of fields in forms
- Making it highly responsive. It's terribly annoying to be clicking on a website continuously and receiving either no response or a delayed response. Users should be able to engage with the website within a matter of seconds.
- Ensuring that it loads in less than 2 seconds. Few people will stick around to wait for your page to load beyond 2 seconds.
- Using a simplistic design. Too much clutter is a major distraction.

Secure

Identity-theft, hackers, and ransomware masterminds stalk the web searching for unsuspecting prey. Your website shouldn't be the pace where they can launch an attack on unsuspecting customers. This is especially true when an e-commerce website has been created. A Secure Socket Layer (SSL) is what most website developers use to protect websites. SSL technology can be purchased from Godaddy SSL, VeriSign.com, Thawte.com or Comodo.

Mobile-Friendly

Most customers will interact with your website from their mobile devices. Therefore, it is prudent to ensure that your website can function on smartphones, tablets, and PCs. This doesn't mean that your mobile website should be completely different from your desktop/PC website. You should create a seamless online experience, not confuse users.

A mobile-friendly website has all of the features previously outlined with the following additions:

- Use high-quality images that are mobile-friendly. Images that are too large can affect load speeds.
- If you use videos, embed YouTube videos instead of uploading videos.
- Use familiar icons.
- Ensure that your business' contact information is easy to locate.
- Any forms that are used should be optimized for mobile.

Choosing to Hire a Web Developer or Perform a DIY

A website is an investment. The type of investment you make depends on your budget and the objectives of your company. The need for websites has increased exponentially over the past decade. Consequently, a variety of website builder sites have been created to facilitate people who want to build their own websites. Some of the most popular website builders are WordPress, BoldGrid, Squarespace, Shopify, Weebly and GoDaddy Website Builder.

Building your website yourself is feasible if you're a freelancer operating alone. It would be more cost-effective to create a simple website that your clients can use to make contact with you and view portfolio samples. On the other hand, it may be more feasible for a larger company to hire a website developer to create a customized website. Website developers aren't cheap but they create websites that support the image of a professional brand.

How to Create Engaging Business Social Media Profiles

Social media has created a global community of individuals who are able to more actively engage with the brands they love. Effective use of social media isn't about creating random posts. Instead, it involves:

- Choosing the right social media platform that best represents your brand.
- Creating the right content
- Keeping followers actively engaged
- Using the right social media marketing tactics

Social Media Platforms

Careful thought must be given to the social media platform(s) used to build your brand's social media identity. LinkedIn, for instance, appeals to an audience that is different from Facebook. The same is true for SnapChat and Twitter. Answering the following questions will help you make the right decision:

1. What is the main social media platform that your target audience uses? If your target audience is 50-year-old business women, for instance, it's highly unlikely that you'll find them on SnapChat.
2. How do you want to tailor your social media profile to reach your target audience? In other words, what is the goal of your platform?
3. What social media platforms do your competitors use? How are they using these platforms? What are the strengths and weaknesses of how they're able to engage their customers? Buzzsumo is a good tool to use to gain invaluable insight into how well your competitor's content is performing.
4. What type of content do you want to share? Professional industry-related content is best shared on LinkedIn. Video content is best shared on Instagram, Vine, SnapChat, or Periscope. Facebook is the leader in live videos. Image-based content is best shared on Instagram or Pinterest.

Social media profiles for businesses can only be effective if at least 2 platforms are used. Sticking to one platform creates a very narrow audience. Using too many platforms, however, will be too much to maintain. Stick to 2 or 3 and you'll be ready to truly set sail. The following social media management tools can help you with scheduling content:

1. Hootsuite
2. Buffer

3. SocialOomph
4. SproutSocial

Creating the Right Content

Humans have a natural desire for variety in all things in life. Your brand's social media profiles should follow suit by using a variety of content. Don't use your brand's social media page exclusively as a promotional tool for your business. Instead, use it as a platform to share content that establishes the company as an expert in the niche. Interspersing promotional material occasionally is okay but it shouldn't be an overwhelming part of what you do.

Additionally, you want to create content that is highly likely to get reactions, shares, and comments. Types of content that could be used in a social media profile include:

- Informative content
- Live content
- Content that evokes emotion
- Humorous content
- Inspirational content
- Content that tells a story

Actively Engaging Followers

Your social media followers are searching for useful content that they can share and start conversations about. The beauty is that you can use content across multiple platforms. For instance, a video that you create for your Facebook account can also be used on your Twitter or Instagram accounts. Some types of content that you can use to actively engage followers include:

- How-to videos
- Behind the scenes videos
- Event videos
- Demonstration videos
- Interviews
- Customer testimonial videos
- Start a Twitter Live Chat
- Attention-grabbing titles for your articles
- Photos
- Polls
- Posts with a clear call-to-action
- Infographics
- Open-ended questions to encourage responses
- Surveys
- Relevant hashtags

Social Media Marketing Tactics

Social media marketing truly benefits businesses when it is done correctly. The following strategies can help you create successful social media marketing campaigns.

- Ensure that your campaign has a goal. Goals have been a major part of what we have been discussing in this book. A social media marketing campaign that doesn't have a goal is like a ship without a map. You can only measure the success of your campaign if it has a goal. An example of a social media marketing campaign goal is given below.
  - o The objective of this campaign is to get more website traffic that converts into paying customers throughout the life of the campaign.

- Use your goal to craft a detailed campaign strategy. Your strategy should answer the following questions:
    o Which of my brand's social media profiles is best suited to accomplish the goal of this campaign?
    o What type of content will I use in the campaign?
    o Will I be running the campaign or will I hire someone to run the campaign?
    o How does this campaign fit into the overall image I'm trying to portray for my brand on social media?
    o What metric will I use to determine if the campaign has been successful? Possible metrics include website traffic stats, amount of engagement, number of people who complete contact forms, number of downloads, or number of purchases.
- Give people a reason to engage with the content of your campaign. This requires using content that would be valuable to your audience.
- Use relevant keywords and hashtags. The right keywords and hashtags can help you reach people outside of your followers. It can even help you reach people outside of the reach of a paid campaign.
- Direct people to the right landing page on your website. The landing page you choose depends on the objective of the campaign. For instance, if your campaign's copy says that the viewer can click the link to make a purchase, the link should direct the user to your sales page, not your home page.
- Actively engage with people who participate in your campaign. Respond to their comments and like their posts. People like to know that they're interacting with a real person who cares about their feedback.

Content Marketing

Content is the heartbeat of social media. There would be no engagement without articles, videos, and images that truly capture interest. Novice entrepreneurs often misunderstand how to create content that that truly appeals to their target audience. Strategies for creating memorable articles and videos are outlined below.

Strategies for Creating Memorable Articles or Blog Posts

1. Know your target-audience. Always remember that you're not writing for yourself; you're writing to appeal to a specific group of people. Think about their needs and interests and how your content can appeal to those needs and interests.

2. Create a catchy headline that isn't longer than 8 words. Some leeway can be given to creating a title that exceeds this limit if more words will create the right impact. The headline should be relevant to the target reader's interest, create the right expectations, clearly show the value that can be added, and include a relevant keyword. It's always a good idea to have several possible titles and choose the title that most resonates with the content you're trying to convey. An example of an appropriate headline for an article about after-school activities for children is, "6 Superstar Activities that Will Make Your Kids Love You to the Moon and Back." Although it exceeds the recommended word-count, it is a title that builds intrigue. A parent looking for activities for her children would think that this article must contain some really fun things to do.

3. Write a captivating introduction. People often won't read beyond the first 2 sentences if these sentences aren't interesting enough. Use the first paragraph to tell a story or joke, evoke empathy, or present interesting statistics. Ensure that the paragraph ends with a clear description of how the article will address a problem the reader could be having.

4. Organize the content into sections so that readers aren't overwhelmed. Large blocks of text can be very intimidating. Divide the text into smaller portions with relevant headings. It's especially useful to create list type articles. For instance, the kids' activities article mentioned above would have 6 activities that the reader should look out for.

5. Fill in the blanks with meaningful content. Remember that your readers are looking for content that adds value.

6. Have a relevant call-to-action at the end of the post.

7. Include relevant links to reputable content that supports your points if applicable.

8. Always edit and proofread your work. You will be tempted to schedule a post immediately after writing without double-checking. After all, you've used so much of your energy creating the article that it's difficult to find additional energy to reread it. However, reviewing what you've written can prevent embarrassment because it helps you ensure that the work you present is free of grammatical, typographical and punctuation errors. It also ensures that you're truly conveying the right message.

9. Use a relevant feature image. Visuals appeal stronger to the human psyche than words. All of your blog posts

should include an image related to the topic that will gain the interest of readers.

10. Include relevant tags for the post.
11. Track the metrics. Pay attention to the engagement your blog posts and articles receive. These metrics provide valuable insight into what really interests your readers and what could be done to tailor future articles.

Strategies for Creating Memorable Videos

1. Know your target audience and the goal of your video.
2. Consider the unique content that your video can offer that is far different from what your competitors offer.
3. Create a compelling title that follows the same guidelines as those presented in the previous section.
4. Create a meaningful and engaging script that appeals to your target audience.
5. Create quality videos. The objective of your video will determine whether or not you can do it yourself or need to hire a professional. However, it should still be a high-quality video if you do choose to perform a DIY. Some possible simple video editing software you can use are iMovie, Windows Movie Maker, and Filmora. The quality is just as important as the content.
6. Use relevant tags and hashtags.
7. Use the engagement data to tailor future videos or edit the existing video.

Chapter 8 Activity

1. Create a website.

2. Choose 2 social media platforms for your brand.
3. Create a one month content marketing strategy for your website and social media platforms using the template below.

Name of Social Media Platform:

Content for Week 1 (Tick All that Apply)

	Type of Content	Amount Needed	Purpose
	Blog article		
	Image post		
	Infographic		
	Newsletter		
	Guide or E-Book		

Content for Week 2 (Tick All that Apply)

	Type of Content	Amount Needed	Purpose
	Blog article		
	Image post		
	Infographic		
	Newsletter		

	Guide or E-Book		

Content for Week 3 (Tick All that Apply)

	Type of Content	Amount Needed	Purpose
	Blog article		
	Image post		
	Infographic		
	Newsletter		
	Guide or E-Book		

Content for Week 4 (Tick All that Apply)

	Type of Content	Amount Needed	Purpose
	Blog article		
	Image post		
	Infographic		
	Newsletter		
	Guide or E-Book		

4. Create a schedule for posting the content you need. Include possible titles for each type of content and how you plan to create and publish the content.

Chapter 9
Market beyond Digital Screens

"Think big and don't listen to people who tell you it can't be done. Life's too short to think small."

Tim Ferris

The rise of digital marketing hasn't made traditional marketing obsolete. Marketing is really about finding creative ways to compel people to buy your products or services. The strongest marketing strategies incorporate both digital and traditional media. However, the reality is that many new entrepreneurs don't have the capital to embark on extensive traditional marketing campaigns. Creative non-digital marketing strategies that can fit within your budget include:

-    Posting flyers on library or community notice boards

-    Planning and hosting a promotional event

-    Sending out a press release to your local paper

-    Low budget newspaper ad space

-    Cross-promotion

Posting Flyers

Talented graphic designers can be hired for very low costs using websites such as Fiverr and 99designs. Hire one of these designers to create a simple poster that showcases your business. Print a few of these posters and post them in public places that your target audience visits.

Planning and Hosting a Promotional Event

Promotional events are good for business if they are well executed. Launch parties, galas, concerts are just a few examples of the types of events that get people excited. It's all about creating a buzz that gets people talking about your business. This creates in a domino effect that opens pathways for you to earn more than what you spent planning the event.

An event planner takes the strain of planning and executing an event away from you so that you can spend more time on fundamental components of your business. However, you may want to forgo hiring an event planner and work with your team to plan the event in order to save money. Regardless of the option you choose, you must be able to answer the following questions.

1. What is the purpose of the event? Do you want to build interest in a new product? Do you want to create an environment for key players in your industry to meet? Do you want to raise funds for charity?

2. What type of event would best suit the purpose?

3. Where is the best place to have the event?

4. Who should be invited to the event? How will these people be invited?

5. What is your budget for the event?

6. Who needs to be hired to make the event successful?

7. How will you determine whether or not the event has been successful?

Sending out a Press Release

A press release provides an official statement about your company to the public. You can use a press release to tell the public more about your product, give details about an upcoming event, or share important information related to your company. It can, however, be difficult to get a press release published. The likelihood of your press release being noticed increases if you follow these tips:

- Send a press release to publications that are interested in what you have to say.

- Ensure that the story is newsworthy. Do research to determine what the publication deems to be noteworthy.

- Write a story that is essentially already ready to publish.

- Ensure that correct grammar, spelling and punctuation are used.

- Be clear and succinct.

Purchasing Low-Budget Newspaper Ad Space

Newspaper ad space doesn't have to be a full or quarter page all color in-your-face ad. There are some lower budget spaces that can still give you the right visibility. Also, consider doing frequent small ads instead of one large ad.

Considering Cross-Promotion

Cross-promotion essentially involves working with other companies to combine marketing efforts. It provides the distinct advantage of allowing both companies to grow through each other's customer base. There are several ways that you can do cross-promotions. Some strategies are highlighted below:

- Mention your partner on social media.

- Write blog articles that include links to your partner company's website.

- Include your partner company in a press release.

- Offer incentives to customers who buy from your partner and vice versa.

- Send combined promotional emails to both your mailing lists.

- Participate in a joint interview with the media.

Cross-promotions work best when there is a referral program in place. Each partner should receive an incentive for referrals. It has to be a win-win partnership. For instance, a printer could collaborate with a paper manufacturer. This company could offer discounts to customers who purchase any of the paper company's products at the printing company. The paper manufacturer could in turn offer the printing company discounts on paper products.

Chapter 9 Activity

1. Which non-digital strategy mentioned in this chapter most interests you? How can you make that strategy a part of your marketing plan?

2. Which company can you collaborate with for a cross-promotion campaign?

Chapter 10
Crunch the Numbers
"Success is the sum of small efforts repeated day in and day out."

R. Colier

Keeping tabs on your business' financials makes you a proactive, instead of reactive, leader. Outstanding invoices, overspending, and discrepancies in cash-flow statements must be caught early to prevent future losses. It is crucial for you to hire an accountant or outsource your accounting to an accounting firm. This chapter outlines how you can keep tabs of your business' finances, determine the market-rate salary to pay employees, know how to invest the business' money, and keep tabs of IRS tax payments. This information is essentially a summary of the principles presented in Greg Crabtree's highly informative book *Simple Numbers, Straight Talk, Big Profits: 4 Keys to Unlock Your Business Potential.* We encourage you to read this book because it will give you valuable insight into the true picture of a profitable business.

Market-Rate Salaries

Some business owners choose to pay whatever salaries they deem appropriate for themselves and their staff, especially during the early stages of a business. This is the wrong approach because it can provide a false picture of the company's profits and lead to employee dissatisfaction. Your business is operating at a loss if you aren't able to pay both yourself and your employees a market-based wage.

Two reputable websites offer up-to-date information about market-based salaries. The first is Economic Research Institute's

Salary Survey Assessor found at www.erieri.com. The second is Salary.com. All you have to do is input the position and salaries across various states will be displayed.

You should never pay yourself a market-based wage if your business truly can't afford it.

One thing that should be made clear though is that you should never pay yourself a market-based wage if your business truly can't afford it. You earn sweat equity instead. Sweat equity is the value you've added to the business with no salary. Your aim should always be to get your business to a point where sweat equity becomes money that you actually earn.

While you can pay yourself sweat equity for a period of time, all of your employees should be paid a market-based salary. One of the pitfalls of not paying employees a market-based salary is high turnover rates. You may think that you are saving the company money by paying low salaries, but high turnover rates cost the company far more. Money has to be spent training replacements and productivity hours are lost while people double up to complete the tasks of the missing person. This inevitably leads to customer dissatisfaction, a poor brand image, and a dip in revenue. Pay employees what they're worth.

Keeping Tabs on the Business' Finances

Pre-tax profit is one of the most important numbers on your income statement. It is simply the profit the business earns before taxes are paid. A business that has a pre-tax profit that is 5 percent or less of its revenue is on the road to destruction. Your aim should always be to keep pre-tax profits at or above 10 percent. More information about factors that affect pre-tax profits can be found.

There are certain financial statements that you must see regularly in order to keep track of your business' pre-tax profit. These financial statements are the daily cash balance, the cash flow forecast report, the sales and productivity report, and the profit and loss report. The cash flow forecast and sales and productivity reports should be viewed either on a weekly or bi-weekly basis. The profit and loss report should be viewed on a monthly basis.

The daily cash balance information lets you know the income that was received that day and how much money is in the business' account after all bills have been paid that day. A low cash balance means that you need to take action before revenue falls to critical levels. The cash flow forecast report shows your expected inflows and outflows for the next 2 weeks. It gives a clear picture of whether or not you will have enough money to pay the bills of the business. The sales and productivity report essentially helps you see how well your sales team is working to gain income for the business. The monthly profit and loss report helps you see the highs and lows for the year and make predictions for future profit. Each of these reports plays an integral role in helping you keep tabs on the amount of money your business is either losing or earning.

Paying Taxes

Don't try to jump through loopholes to avoid paying taxes. The IRS has plans available that allow you to pay taxes quarterly, bi-annually or annually. Speak with an accountant to determine the arrangement that works best for you. Tax payments should be factored into your cash flow forecast. The point is that you shouldn't try to go through the backdoor of tax payments.

Investing the Business' Profits

There will be a point in your business where more than 10 percent of your revenue is pre-tax profits. An urge to splurge will rise within you because you want to keep up with the Joneses. The success of your business is more important than maintaining an image or distributing profits to the owners. This is especially true during the early stages of the business. The profits earned should be put back into the business to improve infrastructure and operations, invest in employees, or invest in marketing. You could even do a combination of all 3 if profits are that good. These investments will help the business flourish and produce even greater profits.

Chapter 10 Activity

1. List all of your current staff members.
2. Identify the market-rate salary for each staff member.
3. Identify a market-rate salary for yourself based on the role you have in the company.
4. Discuss the financial tracking reports outlined in this chapter with your financial officers.
5. Think about ways that you can reinvest future profits into the business.

Chapter 11
Project Growth

"Everyone wants to live on top of the mountain, but all the happiness and growth occurs while you're climbing it."

Andy Rooney

You've been planting the seeds for a successful business over the past 10 chapters. IT's now time to focus on the future of your business. It's your responsibility to create the environment for your business to grow, even in tough economic climates. Growth requires proper planning and a strong team to effectively implement plans.

Creating a 5 Year Plan

A 5 year plan has the following components:

1. A vision
2. Objectives
3. Strategies for accomplishing the objectives
4. Benchmarks to know that the objectives have been fulfilled

Let's look at an example of a 5 year plan for a writing company. You can use this example to create your own 5 year plan.

Vision

Our vision is to become one of the top 5 writing companies in America that offers ghostwriting, copywriting, proofreading and editing services within the next 5 years.

Objectives

We must fulfill the following objectives in order to achieve this vision:

1. We must create a highly-skilled team of the best writers, proofreaders and editors.
2. We must create a reliable website that provides customers with useful guides, eBooks, and payment options for our services.
3. We must increase the number of best-selling non-fiction eBooks we publish each year.
4. We must create an online writing course by the end of the fourth year.
5. We must create a successful You Tube channel by the end of the fifth year.
6. Our pre-tax profits must be at least 16 percent of our revenue by the end of year 5.

Strategies for Accomplishing the Objectives

Objective 1

1. Hire a talent scout to screen and select the best candidates who can commit to full-time work from remote locations.
2. Give each employee a probationary period of 3 months.
3. Establish a quality-assurance department that vets the quality of the work each writer, proofreader and editor produces.

4. Encourage each writer to publish and gauge the success of his or her own eBook.

Objective 2

1. Hire a web developed to create a high-quality website that has space for inclusion of free and paid material, courses, and videos.
2. Ensure that all measures are in place to facilitate safe payment for services.
3. Ensure that a web developer is on staff to maintain the website.

Objective 3

1. Have regular strategic planning meetings to discuss the latest strategies for making an eBook a best-seller.
2. Ensure that each eBook a client requests has a team of individuals who can write, edit, proofread, and market the book.
3. Consistently analyze marketing strategies to identify what works and what doesn't work.
4. Hire a computer programmer to develop a program that tracks the success of all the eBooks we publish.

Objective 4

1. Accumulate enough material over the 5 year period to create the online writing course.
2. Use the right platform to create the course and link it to our website.
3. Market the course.
4. Track how the course generates leads for the business.

Objective 5

1. Accumulate enough material over the 5 year period to create a You Tube channel.
2. Buy the right equipment to create high-quality videos.
3. Hire a video editor to make the videos the right quality.
4. Track the success of each video.

Objective 6

1. Keep track of all the revenue obtained from all streams of income.
2. Keep track of daily, weekly and monthly income using the appropriate reports.
3. Modify streams of income that aren't generating profit.

Benchmarks for Success

1. Client feedback indicates that we have a highly-skilled team of the best writers, proofreaders and editors.
2. A reliable and effective website is created.
3. The number of best-selling non-fiction books increases each year.
4. An online writing course that has active and engaged participants is created.
5. A You Tube channel with over 200 subscribers is created.
6. Our pre-tax profits are at least 16 percent of our revenue by the end of year 5.

Knowing When to Expand Your Business

The first signs of success may make you think that it's time to put your business in overdrive. However, trying to expand too soon can severely affect your bottom-line and even force our business to close. You know it's time to expand your business when you have the right systems in place, you have the cash-flow to support an expansion, you have a strong team, and you have a loyal customer base.

The Right Systems

Your business has to be in a place to support expansion. You will need new staff, a distribution strategy, somewhere to store inventory, and a way to ensure consistency at each location. O you have the manpower, money and equipment to accomplish all 3 feats?

Cash-Flow

Profits have to be really good over a period of time to support expansion. You can't look at this month's profits and use that as your benchmark for expansion. Watch your profits grow over the next 2 to 3 years before jumping into expansion.

Inventory Storage

You may need to outsource inventory storage as you expand. Demand for your products may mean that you're bursting at the seams with no place to put everything. Sort out where you're going to put everything before making the leap to expand.

Strong Team

Business expansion tests the mettle of a team. Longer ours are going to be required. You're going to have to relinquish control of certain aspects of your business to your management team. Do you trust them enough to get the job done? Can they train new staff for your new location? Are they ready for the big move?

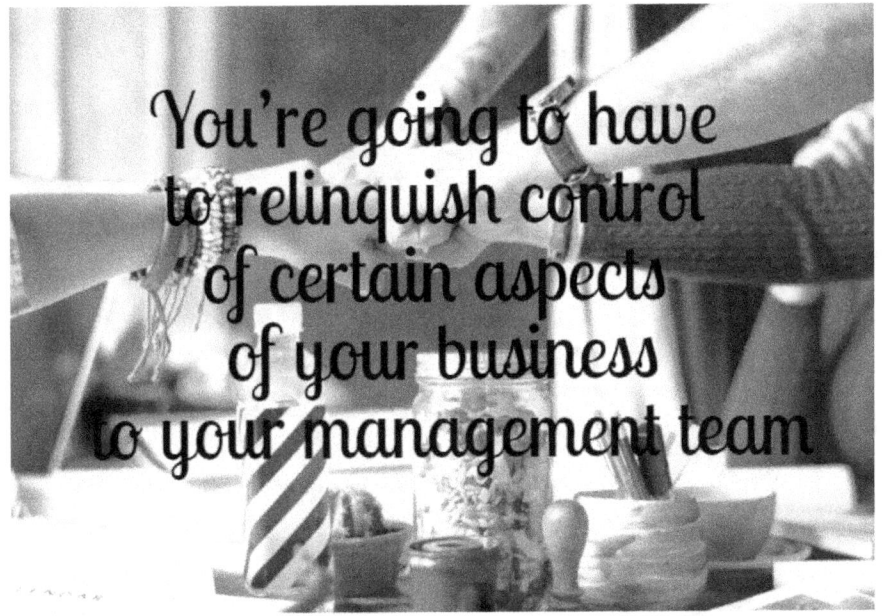

You're going to have to relinquish control of certain aspects of your business to your management team

Loyal Customer Base

At the end of the day, everything boils down to your customers. It makes no sense expanding a business if there are insufficient customers to support it. Make sure that you have customer support before making the move.

Chapter 11 Activity

1. Create a 5 year plan for your business.

2. Have an idea of when you may want to expand your business. Ensure that you have measures in place to support this expansion when the time is right.

Chapter 12
Become a Champion for Others
"Women who support other women are confident, generous visionaries."

Mariela Dabbah

Too often we view each other as threats instead of allies. We paint a picture of the whole world being against us. The only way to get ahead in some women's eyes is to trample on other women. There is power in one woman, but there is even greater power in many women.

This book has empowered you to take the leap of faith and create your own business. You now have a responsibility to help other women do the same. This chapter outlines 5 ways that you can be a champion for other women.

Speak with a United Front

Some women's voices go unheard. More strength can be added to their message by more women speaking out about the same issues. Support other the ideas and viewpoints of other women who you agree with. If there is a cause to fight for, join other women in the fight for the cause.

Create More Opportunities for Women in Higher-Level Positions

Create opportunities for women to grown in your business. Offer them promotions, further training opportunities, and mentorship. Don't let the brilliance of a woman threaten you. Support that brilliance. Treat all women fairly by providing them with the same opportunities that you would provide their male counterparts.

Promote Other Female Businesses

There are so many female-owned businesses in America. Support these businesses by purchasing their products and recommending them to your friends and family. You can even use your business' social media pages to send them a shout out. Help them get their business in front of more eyes.

Offer Training Opportunities

Reach out to women in your community to provide mentorship and training opportunities. There are women in the present workforce who need to upgrade their technology skills. There are also women who want to take the leap into entrepreneurship but don't have the knowledge to take the first step. Be the support they need to at least find the right path.

Examples of Women Helping Other Women Succeed

Sheryl Sandberg, COO of Facebook

Sheryl Sandberg created the book *Lean In: Women, Work and the Will to Lead* after her 2012 TED talk about ways women are held back. She created this book to shed light on the harsh realities faced b women in business and inspire more women to change the dynamic. This book has created a "Lean-In Movement" led by the Sheryl Sandberg and Dave Goldberg Family Foundation. Chief among the initiatives of this Foundation is leanin.org, an organization that brings women from all over the world together.

Leanin.org's mission is to "empower women to achieve their ambitions." They do this by creating Lean-In Circles which "are small peer groups that meet regularly to learn and grow together." It is an initiative that can be found in cities worldwide. The organization also has an annual public awareness campaign to shed light on issues affecting women. Finally, they produce an annual study about women in the workplace and offer free learning resources.

Adriana Gascoige, Founder of Girls in Tech

Technology is an industry in which women are the most underrepresented. Adriana created Girls in Tech to change that dynamic by encouraging more women to become tech entrepreneurs. She achieves this objective by hosting boot camps, hackathons, pitch competitions, and virtual classrooms.

Vicki Saunders, Founder of SheEO

SheEO's mission is to provide more opportunities for financing and supporting female-led businesses. It is funded through a community of women, called Activators, who contribute $1,100 annually. This money is pooled together and 5 female-led ventures chosen by the Activators are given low interest 5-year loans from the pool of funds. This creates a continuous pool of funds. All members of the organization receive support through monthly coaching and a team of mentors.

Melisa Lin, Founder of Nommery

Nommery puts an interesting twist on social networking events. Women can connect with other women in fine-dining experiences in the San Francisco Bay Area. Users can either attend an event hosted by Nommery or invite people to their own fine-dining event. Melisa has found a great way to encourage women to network with each other.

Chapter 12 Activity

1. List 3 ways that you can support women in your community.
2. What do you need to do to provide this support?
3. Set a goal to help at least one female employee or female entrepreneur this week

Conclusion

You are a powerful, beautiful woman. It's time to hold your head up high and stride into your destiny like a B.O.S.S. The business world is a tough world to be in, but you can overcome all the obstacles thrown your way by following the 12 strategies outlined in this book. Each chapter discussed a strategy and provided you with actionable tips for successful execution.

Women in business face unique challenges. Some of the challenges were described in this book. However, the truth is that life is unpredictable and there may be challenges that you face that we haven't mentioned. Regardless of what comes your way, you can still emerge a winner if you have the right team and network of women to support you. Keep the lyrics of Alicia Keys' hit song *Superwoman* embedded in your mind. You are a superwoman all day, every day. Cheers to your success!